My Recovery Road Media Group

A Journey of Surrender

12 STEPS + 12 SONGS + 1 HIGHER POWER

Song Analysis Workbook

Songs and Song Analysis by Rev. John Lippard

Curriculum by Rev. Bridget Lippard

Companion to the Music Album

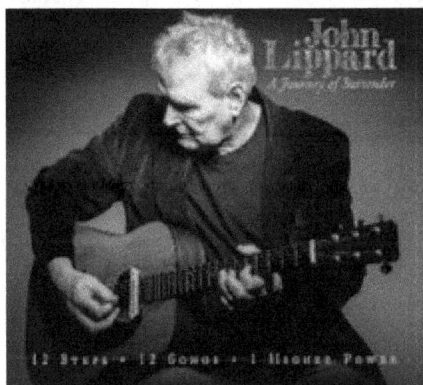

Music Album digitally
available at:

johnlippard.com

myrecoveryroad.com

Songs and Song Analysis Rev. John Lippard

Curriculum Rev. Bridget Lippard

Cover Photo Rachel Corlew-Hodges

The 12 Steps to New Life

This book is not affiliated with or endorsed by Alcoholics Anonymous. The 12 Steps to New Life are a faith-based adaptation inspired by the spiritual principles of the original Twelve Steps and are presented within a Christ-centered framework.

Bible Scripture Versions

To the One who made a way where there was none, Jesus Christ, our Savior and our Strength.

To our mothers, whose prayers carried us through the darkest nights, whose love never wavered, whose faith never faltered.

This book is dedicated to both of you. You are the reason we are here, the reason we are whole, the reason we found our way back to God.

Thank you.

And to the souls who are still searching for a way out, never give up hope, our prayers are with you. There is a path to freedom, and it starts with one step at a time.

Contents

12 Steps to New Life

Step One

Admitting we can't overcome addiction on our own, we are powerless and choose to depend on Jesus for strength.

Step Two

Believing that Jesus Christ can restore our lives, renew our minds, and bring hope where addiction once ruled.

Step Three

Choosing to surrender our will and our lives to Jesus, trusting Him to lead us in a new way forward.

Step Four

Taking an honest and courageous look within, inviting God to reveal our patterns, wounds, and places that need healing.

Step Five

Admitting the truth about our struggles to God, to ourselves, and to someone we trust, allowing honesty to open the door to healing.

Step Six

Becoming willing for God to transform our hearts and remove attitudes, habits, and behaviors that no longer align with His will.

Step Seven

Humbly asking Jesus to heal our wounds, strengthen our character, and restore what addiction has damaged.

Step Eight

Becoming willing to make things right by making a list of those we have harmed, as God prepares our hearts for reconciliation.

Step Nine

Making amends wherever possible, guided by love, wisdom, and humility, without causing further harm.

Step Ten

Continuing daily self-reflection, promptly admitting wrongs and returning quickly to God when we fall short.

Step Eleven

Growing in our relationship with God through prayer and Scripture, seeking His guidance, peace, and power each day.

Step Twelve

Living out this new freedom by helping others, sharing hope, and walking forward in a transformed life with Christ.

The Serenity Prayer

God, grant me the serenity
to accept the things I cannot change,
courage to change the things I can,
and wisdom to know the difference.

A Prayer of Surrender (Inspired Reflection)

God, help me live one day at a time and trust You in each moment.
Teach me to walk through hardship without losing peace.
Help me accept this world as it is while surrendering my will to Yours.
I trust that You are at work—today and forever—
shaping true joy in this life and eternal hope in the life to come.

Introduction

No matter where you are in your recovery journey, whether in the early stages or walking in long-term freedom, the principles found in the 12 Steps have proven to be timeless tools for overcoming life's struggles. I know personally the devastation addiction can bring, and it was through the 12 Steps that I discovered the necessity of a Higher Power. For me, that Higher Power is Jesus Christ, who has faithfully guided me through more than forty years of recovery.

In my life, I have been blessed with many titles including songwriter, singer, worship leader, author, and ordained minister. In this project, God has used the gift of songwriting to give voice to His words, expressing the struggles, surrender, and hope experienced by His children walking through addiction and recovery. These songs, born out of time alone with God and deep reflection, stand as my personal testimony to a faith based recovery journey. They reflect the heart behind the 12 Steps to New Life, a Christ centered adaptation of the original spiritual principles, offered here as a pathway of surrender, healing, and transformation through the power of music and the restoring work of God in my life.

The 12 Steps through Song

[18] *Don't be drunk with wine, because that will ruin your life. Instead, be filled with the Holy Spirit,* [19] *singing psalms and hymns and spiritual songs among yourselves and making music to the Lord in your hearts.* [20] *And give thanks for everything to God the Father in the name of our Lord Jesus Christ.* Ephesians 5:18-20 (NLT)

This Bible verse is a coping strategy for those in recovery, it encourages them to look at something bigger and outside of ourselves for help. And to have a support group to turn to when struggling.

Scripture reminds us not to be drunk with wine, but instead to be filled with the Spirit, expressing our hearts through songs. What a powerful coping skill and recovery practice. Just as the Twelve Steps have become a widely recognized language of recovery, music has long been known as a universal language of the soul. Recovery research has shown that music, when combined with step based principles, can be a meaningful addition to the recovery tool kit for those walking the road of healing and freedom. The music album *A Journey of Surrender: 12 Steps + 12 Songs + 1 Higher Power* builds on these truths by pairing music with the **12 Steps to New Life**, a Christ centered adaptation of the original step principles that invites listeners into surrender and restoration through faith in God.

Each song corresponds to one step in the journey toward surrendering to God as one's Higher Power, reflecting the heart and progression of the **12 Steps to New Life**. Through soulful melodies and heartfelt lyrics, listeners are gently led by the Holy Spirit through a process of healing, growth, and renewal. From recognizing powerlessness to seeking God's guidance and direction, the album illustrates a path of surrender and faith, offering a musical expression of the step journey as it unfolds through a Christ centered recovery lens.

Song Analysis

The Song Analysis workbook is a companion to "A Journey of Surrender" music album. Song analysis can be a powerful tool for identifying and processing emotions, as it offers a way to connect with one's feelings through the themes, words, and musical elements of a song. This tool serves as a mirror allowing a person to see their emotions reflected back at them in a safe, non-judgmental way. This process helps individuals get in touch with their feelings, validate their emotions, release built-up tension, and gain clarity on how to process and cope with difficult emotions.

History of the 12 Steps of Alcoholics Anonymous

The Twelve Steps of Alcoholics Anonymous (A.A.) have become one of the most influential and widely practiced frameworks for addiction recovery worldwide. The Steps were originally formulated by Bill Wilson, a co-founder of A.A., drawing from his personal spiritual experience and from the moral and spiritual principles of the Oxford Group—an early twentieth-century Christian movement that emphasized personal transformation through self-examination, confession, restitution, surrender to God, and service to others.

The Twelve Steps were first published in 1939 in *Alcoholics Anonymous: The Story of How More Than One Hundred Men Have Recovered from Alcoholism*. In the earliest years of the fellowship, particularly in Akron and Cleveland, Ohio, recovery efforts were deeply shaped by these spiritual practices. According to historian Dick B., who extensively documented the spiritual roots of early A.A., accounts from this period describe unusually high levels of sustained sobriety among those who fully embraced these principles (Dick B., *The Akron Genesis of Alcoholics Anonymous*; *The Oxford Group and Alcoholics Anonymous*). While exact success rates from this era cannot be independently verified, the testimonies and records preserved from early members point to a profound pattern of transformation during A.A.'s formative years.

Many of A.A.'s early pioneers personally understood their recovery through a distinctly Christian framework. Dick B. notes that early members frequently interpreted alcoholism not only as a physical and emotional struggle, but as a spiritual condition requiring surrender, repentance, and spiritual renewal (Dick B., *The Good Book and the Big Book*). For these individuals, faith in Jesus Christ was central to their understanding of healing and restoration. Although this Christ-centered perspective played a significant role in the movement's early development, A.A. later broadened its language to welcome people of diverse beliefs while preserving the spiritual foundation of the Steps.

Meetings held in the early days of A.A., including those hosted in Dr. Bob Smith's home in Akron, would have closely resembled Christian home fellowship gatherings of the time. Dick B. documents that these meetings commonly included periods of quiet reflection or meditation, prayer, Bible reading, the use of Oxford Group devotional materials, and the sharing of personal testimonies describing life change and renewed hope (Dick B., *The Akron Genesis of Alcoholics Anonymous*). These practices fostered a communal environment centered on honesty, humility, and spiritual growth.

Prayer and meditation were especially emphasized as daily disciplines. Clarence Snyder, one of the early A.A. pioneers, is often credited with teaching those he sponsored the principle that "prayer is talking to God; meditation is listening to God." Dick B. records that many early members testified that incorporating these practices into their daily lives was essential to maintaining sobriety and spiritual stability (Dick B., *New Light on Alcoholism*). Over time, these disciplines were formally embedded in the Eleventh Step, shaping the spiritual rhythm that continues to guide recovery within A.A. today.

Lectio Divina

Lectio Divina is a spiritual practice, it is a process of reading, reflecting, responding, and resting upon the Word of God. The concept of Lectio Divina dates to the 3rd Century Church and credited to *Origen of Alexandria*, a Christian scholar and theologian.

Lectio Divina is not a Bible study, nor is it reading the entire Bible in a year, it is a simple practice. Lectio Divina starts with one scripture that speaks to you. This is not about rushing through words, but about slowing down and really letting each word of the scripture soak in. Then, take some time to reflect on what you've read. What does it mean for you? How can you apply it to your life? You will find that one word or a phrase will be highlighted by the Holy Spirit for you to meditate on.

To begin, find a place and time (mornings are good for most people) where you are alone and comfortable. Ask the Holy Spirit to quiet your mind from all those things you have going on and ask Him to reveal what scripture you need to mediate on. Remember this isn't a Bible Study so a verse or two is best.

To begin find a favorite scripture, a promise from God (i.e., Jeremiah 29:11). On page 118 is a breakdown of scriptures in categories of things you might be going through, experiencing fear, brokenness, anxiety, finances, etc. and several blank worksheets for you to use.

With each of the Steps there will be a suggested scripture for you to use that goes along with the Step and Song.

By engaging with reflective exercises, insightful song analysis, Lectio Divina and practical tools, you will not only gain a deeper connection to the spiritual principles of recovery but also find tangible ways to apply the 12 Steps in your daily life.

At the end of this journey, you will experience the life-changing power of surrender, discovering lasting peace, and uncovering a new sense of purpose and strength. You will have cultivated a deeper spiritual connection, gained practical insights for personal growth, and embraced the transformative journey of recovery that will continue to guide you long after you complete the course.

Ready to begin the musical journey of surrender through the 12 Steps?

How to Use This Workbook

Listen to each song.

Read the **Key Themes** and take time to reflect and answer the questions.

If in a Small Group Setting discuss the key themes and have the group answer the questions, do not pressure anyone in the group who may not feel comfortable in sharing. And the leader needs to keep a time limit for those who feel comfortable in sharing.

Spend 5 Minutes in Prayer and Meditation for **Lectio Divina,** then follow through with **Action Steps** and the **Closing Prayer**.

Suggested pace for this workbook, one step and one song at a time.

Materials needed: Media Player (i.e., phone, cd player, or computer), Song Analysis Workbook and Bible.

Step One

Admitting we can't overcome addiction on our own, we are powerless and choose to depend on Jesus for strength.

Romans 5:6,8 (AMPC)

*⁶ While we were still helpless [**powerless** to provide for our salvation], at the right time Christ died [as a substitute] for us. ⁸ But God shows and clearly proves **His [own] love** for us by the fact that while we were still sinners, Christ (the Messiah) died for us.*

Powerless

A fatherless child... an angry heart

An abandoned soul... alone in the dark

Wondering how he fell so far into despair

The only way he copes... is to disappear in a high

And pray to God... to let him die

And if he died would anyone really care?

A molested child... a broken heart

Walking the streets...alone in the dark

Her body is all she has left to sell!

Bruised and in pain... life out of control

With no way out... her enslaved soul

Cries, "I can't continue this road to hell"

If you've got nothing to lose...

You've got two options to choose...

Stay the same, or make a change

And admit that you're powerless...over the pain and addictions

You're powerless... over the scars and afflictions

You're powerless... over that life you can't control

You're powerless... over that hunger in your soul... admit that you're powerless

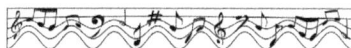

Key Themes and Song Analysis

This song highlights the key themes of brokenness, control, surrender, vulnerability and admitting powerlessness. The key themes are:

Pain and Trauma: The lyrics in Powerless, captures the deep effects of pain and trauma on people's lives. The song depicts individuals who are deeply wounded, highlighting experiences such as abandonment, abuse, neglect, and addiction. The references to a *"fatherless child," "molested child,"* and *"broken heart"* illustrate the emotional and psychological scars these individuals carry.

Can you identify with the life experiences of the individuals in this song? If so, which ones?

How has your life experiences added to your emotional and psychological scares?

Isolation and Despair: Both the characters in the song feel deeply alone *"alone in the dark"*, with their trauma leading them to question their worth and existence *"wondering how he fell so far into despair," "cries, 'I can't continue this road to hell.'*This isolation leads to a sense of hopelessness.

Can you reflect on a time, that your addiction caused you to feel deep despair, hopeless and isolated?

How did those feelings of despair, hopelessness and isolation impact your sense of worth and your perception of life and your future?

Addiction and Escape: The song references the destructive coping mechanisms the individuals turn to, such as drug use *"disappear in a high"* and self-destructive behaviors *"her body is all she has left to sell."* This indicates a theme of escapism as a way to numb the pain and avoid confronting the deep emotional wounds.

What were some deep emotional wounds that you wanted to numb?

What was some self-destructive behaviors that you did to escape reality?

What might be the possible path to healing or breaking free from the vicious cycle?

Powerlessness and Surrender: The repeated phrase *"you're powerless"* underscores a central theme of helplessness in the face of life's struggles. The song emphasizes that the individuals cannot control their pain, addictions, or past traumas on their own, and it suggests the importance of admitting this powerlessness as a first step toward healing.

What pain, addictions or trauma do you feel that you cannot control on you own?

Have you admitted that you are powerless over the things you can't control?

Choice and Change: Despite the overwhelming despair and pain, the song presents a pivotal moment of choice: *"If you've got nothing to lose,* *you've got two options to choose—stay the same or make a change."* This speaks to the possibility of transformation, suggesting that acknowledging one's powerlessness could open the door to recovery and change.

The choice to change creates a hope for transformation and recovery through the acknowledgment of powerlessness. The choice to stay the same eliminates any hope of overcoming despair and pain and the vicious cycle of addiction.

What factors might influence your decisions to stay the same?

What factors might influence your decision to make a change?

Hope for Redemption: While the song explores deep suffering, it ultimately points to the potential for change and redemption. Admitting powerlessness, while painful, could lead to a path of healing and self-improvement, suggesting that individuals can overcome their past and the pain that controls them.

We end this session with one more opportunity for you to admit that you are powerless over your pain and addictions, if you haven't already.

Make a list of things that you need to admit that you're powerless over?

In summary, the song explores themes of trauma, addiction, isolation, and the overwhelming sense of powerlessness. Yet, it also offers a glimmer of hope, highlighting the potential for change and redemption if individuals are willing to face their pain and make a conscious choice to change.

Lectio Divina

Prayer is Talking to God   *Meditation is Listening to God*

Romans 5:6,8 (AMPC)

*⁶ While we were still help less [**powerless** to provide for our salvation], at the right time Christ died [as a substitute] for us. ⁸ But God shows and clearly proves **His [own] love** for us by the fact that while we were still sinners, Christ (the Messiah) died for us.*

Read the verse slowly and focus on each sentence. Re-read the verse a few times and try to notice different words or phrases as they jump out to you.

Reflect and meditate, take a few minutes to sit and be in that moment. Listen for that still small Voice, are there any words speaking to you?

Respond in prayer to what you heard from God and how the words spoke to you. This could be a scripture that you are praying and taking God at His word.

Rest and sit in the silence and just "be" with God for a few minutes. Write down anything that you may have heard during this time resting in His presence. It could be a promise, assurance of a matter being taken care of, a word, etc.

Action Step

Today, I will acknowledge how my addiction controls me and that I am unable to manage my life by myself, accepting the possibility of God offering support and guidance.

Closing Prayer

After spending time in meditation (listening to God) write a prayer to God.

Step Two

Believing that Jesus Christ can restore our lives, renew our minds, and bring hope where addiction once ruled.

John 20:31 (AMP)

but these have been written so that you may believe [with a deep, abiding trust] that Jesus is the Christ (the Messiah, the Anointed), the Son of God; and that by believing [and trusting in and relying on Him] you may have life in His Name.

I Believe

I'd hit rock bottom I was torn to the bone

Scattered and broken with a heart of stone

I'd lost my sanity I didn't recognize myself

When a stranger told me about a Power that could help

If there's a power that is greater than me? Oh, oh I believe!

And if this power can restore my sanity? Oh, oh I believe!

Through it all I'd thrown caution to the wind

I was running hard down that long road of sin

In all the confusion, frustration, and strife'

I thought this Power just might change my life

If there's a power that is greater than me? Oh, oh I believe!

And if this power can restore my sanity? Oh, oh I believe!

Key Themes and Song Analysis

This song reflects a personal struggle with emotional and mental broken-ness that ends with a belief in a power (God) that can bring transformation, redemption and recovery. The key themes are:

Personal Struggle and Despair: The lyrics describe a person who has hit *"rock bottom,"* feeling emotionally and mentally broken *"torn to the bone,"* *"heart of stone."* This suggests a deep sense of loss, pain, and inner turmoil, possibly stemming from life's challenges or poor choices. When someone hits rock bottom it can have different results. It can put you on a path to recovery or it can put you on a path to further descent into addiction. The choice is yours!

Have you hit rock bottom?

If so, describe the experience and the impact it had on your life.

Hope and Transformation: The mention of a *"Power"* that could help and restore sanity indicates a theme of hope and the possibility of change. The individual, initially feeling lost and disconnected from themselves, is introduced to a force greater than themselves that could bring healing.

What was your initial response when you first heard about a power that could help?

Did you believe or did you doubt?

How did your first response effect your life?

Faith and Belief: The repeated phrase "*I believe*" emphasizes the theme of faith—faith in something greater than the self that can provide strength, healing, and sanity. The song reflects a spiritual awakening, where the individual acknowledges a higher power that can guide them toward recovery and self-restoration.

Describe a time if you ever felt a deep longing for something greater than yourself, something that could mend your broken heart and bring you back to wholeness?

What does it mean to truly believe in something bigger than yourself, and how does that belief translate into action?

Can faith truly provide strength, healing, and sanity, and if so, how can you nurture and grow this type of faith?

Redemption and Recovery: The final verses describe a past marked by *"sin," "confusion,"* and *"frustration,"* but there's an underlying sense that the Power (God) has the potential to change the individual's life. This suggests themes of redemption, recovery, and the possibility of personal growth and salvation.

How does acknowledging a power greater than yourself (God), contribute to your personal growth and salvation?

How did your past experiences of *'sin,' 'confusion,'* and *'frustration'* shape your journey toward this transformative change?

In summary, the song captures a journey from despair to hope, with a focus on faith, redemption, and the transformative power of belief in something greater.

Lectio Divina

John 20:31 (AMP)

but these have been written so that you may believe [with a deep, abiding trust] that Jesus is the Christ (the Messiah, the Anointed), the Son of God; and that by believing [and trusting in and relying on Him] you may have life in His Name.

Read the verse slowly and focus on each sentence. Re-read the verse a few times and try to notice different words or phrases as they jump out to you.

Reflect and meditate, take a few minutes to sit and be in that moment. Listen for that still small Voice, are there any words speaking to you?

Respond in prayer to what you heard from God and how the words spoke to you. This could be a scripture that you are praying and taking God at His word.

Rest and sit in the silence and just "be" with God for a few minutes. Write down anything that you may have heard during this time resting in His presence. It could be a promise, assurance of a matter being taken care of, a word, etc.

Action Step

Take some time each day to reflect on how God's power can help you find peace and clarity.

Closing Prayer

Spend a few quiet minutes reflecting on a time when you felt truly lost and hopeless, and then write a prayer for God's strength and guidance to help you find your way back to peace.

Step Three

Choosing to surrender our will and our lives to Jesus, trusting Him to lead us in a new way forward.

Matthew 11:28 (NLT) & 1 John 3:1a (ERV)

Then Jesus said, "Come to me, all of you who are weary and carry heavy burdens, and I will give you rest.

The Father has loved us so much! We are called children of God. ....we really are His children.

Nothing to Lose

God here I am, I'm high again

I know I need You, but don't know where to begin

I've prayed for You to let me die

Now I'm asking You to take control of my life

I've got nothing left; I've got nothing to lose

I'm giving my will and my life to You

Will You be the Father? That I've never known

Will You protect me, and never leave me alone

I'm turning my life over to Your control

Will You have mercy on my abandoned soul

I've got nothing left; I've got nothing to lose

I'm giving my will and my life to You

God here I am, with dirty hands

Don't know how to reach You, help me understand

I've walked these streets so long I don't know myself

I'm crying out to You; I need Your help

I've got nothing left; I've got nothing to lose

I'm giving my will and my life to You

Will You be the Father that I've always dreamed of

and not make me perform, to receive Your love

I'm turning my life over to Your control...

Will You have mercy on my molested soul?

I've got nothing left, I've got nothing to lose,

I'm giving my will and my life to You

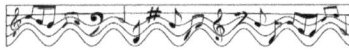

Key Themes and Song Analysis

This song reflects deep emotional themes centered on vulnerability, surrender, and a desperate longing for healing and connection. The key themes are:

Brokenness and Despair: The lyrics express a state of being at rock bottom, with phrases like *"I've got nothing left; I've got nothing to lose"* and references to personal pain, addiction, and feeling abandoned.

What personal pain, (i.e,) abuse, rejection, feelings of abandonment etc.,) contributed to your journey of addiction?

What did you lose in your active addiction?

What was the turning point that turned you toward recovery?

Surrender and Submission: There is a clear theme of relinquishing control, seen in *"I'm giving my will and my life to You"* and the repeated pleas for God to take over and guide the writer.

How does relinquishing control of your life to a higher power (God) influence your journey toward healing and redemption?

When you surrender your will and your life to God, what would be some things you would want Him to restore?

What would be some things that you would want Him to take away?

Yearning for Divine Connection: The song conveys a deep desire for a personal relationship with God, asking for protection, mercy, and unconditional love: *"Will You be the Father that I've always dreamed of?"*

In what ways might this quest for a divine relationship influence your journey toward healing and fulfillment?

The characters in the song are looking for protection, mercy and unconditional love. What are you looking for in a relationship with God?

Seeking Healing and Redemption: The writer longs for healing from past trauma *"Will You have mercy on my molested soul?"* and seeks a fresh start through faith.

What does a fresh start through faith, look like to you, and how would a fresh start influence your path to recovery?

What pain or trauma do you need God to heal?

Themes of Fatherhood and Love: A longing for a nurturing, protective, and unconditionally loving figure is evident, as the writer asks for a Father who won't demand performance in exchange for love.

How might this longing for a supportive and loving Father influence your journey toward healing and emotional fulfillment?

Faith Amid Struggle: Though overwhelmed by pain and doubt, there's a glimmer of faith in turning to God and asking for help, indicating hope for transformation.

With a glimmer of hope in God, what would you ask for to help in your healing and transformation?

What would you do if your faith to believe for healing and transformation didn't produce the results you were hoping for?

Overall, the song is a raw, heartfelt prayer of vulnerability, repentance, and hope, rooted in a deep need for divine intervention and unconditional love. It resonates as both a personal cry and a universal plea for grace and healing.

Lectio Divina

Matthew 11:28 (NLT) & 1 John 3:1a (ERV)

Then Jesus said, "Come to me, all of you who are weary and carry heavy burdens, and I will give you rest.

The Father has loved us so much! We are called children of God. .... we really are His children.

Read the verse slowly and focus on each sentence. Re-read the verse a few times and try to notice different words or phrases as they jump out to you.

Reflect and meditate, take a few minutes to sit and be in that moment. Listen for that still small Voice, are there any words speaking to you?

Respond in prayer to what you heard from God and how the words spoke to you. This could be a scripture that you are praying and taking God at His word.

Rest and sit in the silence and just "be" with God for a few minutes. Write down anything that you may have heard during this time resting in His presence. It could be a promise, assurance of a matter being taken care of, a word, etc.

Action Step

Take a moment to reflect on how God is actively working in your life and acknowledge His presence.

Closing Prayer

Write a prayer admitting your powerless and surrendering to Jesus as your Higher Power.

Step Four

Taking an honest and courageous look within, inviting God to reveal our patterns, wounds, and places that need healing.

Proverbs 20:27 (TLB) & John 16:13a (NLT)

*A man's spirit is the **Lord's searchlight exposing his hidden motives**.*

*However, when He, the **Spirit of truth**, has come, **He will guide you into all truth**, for He will not speak from Himself; but whatever He hears (from the Father), He will speak.*

Looking Inside

Reluctant and fearful I turned my eyes,

into the hollow darkness inside...

I had to see what was haunting me

I'd lost sight of life years ago,

and I had lost complete control...

I've got to find some sanity

The first thing I saw was a heart of stone,

from all the failures that I have known...

while trying to escape reality

Looking deeper I saw the scars,

that comes from not knowing who You are

I became someone I wasn't meant to be

I'm looking inside, I don't like what I see

I've got to make a change!

I'm looking inside, I don't recognize me

I just can't stay the same... I've got to change!

I saw selfish greed taking what wasn't mine

stealing anything that I could find

to get another high to numb the pain.

I saw raging anger ready to destroy

every relationship and steal every joy...

leaving me to deal with the shame.

I'm looking inside, I don't like what I see

I've got to make a change!

I'm looking inside, I don't recognize me

I just can't stay the same... I've got to change!

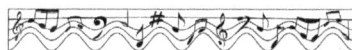

Key Themes and Song Analysis

This song explores themes of self-reflection, regret, and the desire for transformation. The lyrics paint a raw and introspective journey into the writer's inner world of chaos. The key themes are:

Self-Reflection and Awareness: The writer confronts their inner darkness, recognizing personal flaws, pain, and the consequences of their actions. Lines like *"I'm looking inside, I don't like what I see"* highlight this theme. Take a few minutes to self-reflect on your personal flaws, pain, and the consequences of your actions.

What did your self-reflection expose in your inner darkness? Be honest!

What caused you to change when you were in active addiction?

Loss of Identity: A recurring idea is the loss of self, as seen in *"I don't recognize me"* and *"I became someone I wasn't meant to be."* This reflects a longing to rediscover their true identity.

Describe the person you became during your active addiction.

What factors contributed to the loss of your true self?

Despair and Emotional Pain: The lyrics acknowledge deep-seated emotional wounds, failures, and coping mechanisms, such as *"trying to escape reality"* and *"stealing anything that I could find to numb the pain."*

What failures and bad coping mechanisms made you want to escape reality?

What deep-seated emotional wounds caused you to want to numb the pain?

Consequences of Unhealthy Coping: The song details the damage caused by selfishness, addiction, and anger, which lead to shame and broken relationships: *"leaving me to deal with the shame."*

What are some of the unhealthy behaviors that you did in active addiction that caused shame and broken relationships?

How did you respond to the shame your actions caused?

Longing for Change and Redemption: The refrain emphasizes a powerful yearning for transformation: *"I just can't stay the same... I've got to change!"* This theme underscores hope amid despair. The only hope that a person in active addiction has, is that change is possible, if you want it.

How did this longing for change influence your path toward redemption and personal growth?

What additional changes do you feel that you need to make to redeem relationships and undo your shame?

Spiritual Undertones: While not explicitly addressed, the mention of *"not knowing who You are"* suggests a deeper search for meaning, possibly spiritual, and a desire to reconnect with a higher purpose or divine identity.

Describe who you became in your active addiction?

What do you feel you need to do to become who you were meant to be?

This song captures the internal struggle of confronting one's flaws and past while holding onto the hope of change, making it both deeply personal and universally relatable.

Lectio Divina

Proverbs 20:27 (TLB) & John 16:13a (NLT)

*A man's spirit is the **Lord's searchlight exposing his hidden motives**.*

*However, when He, the **Spirit of truth**, has come, **He will guide you into all truth**, for He will not speak from Himself; but whatever He hears (from the Father), He will speak.*

Read the verse slowly and focus on each sentence. Re-read the verse a few times and try to notice different words or phrases as they jump out to you.

Reflect and meditate, take a few minutes to sit and be in that moment. Listen for that still small Voice, are there any words speaking to you?

Respond in prayer to what you heard from God and how the words spoke to you. This could be a scripture that you are praying and taking God at His word.

Rest and sit in the silence and just "be" with God for a few minutes. Write down anything that you may have heard during this time resting in His presence. It could be a promise, assurance of a matter being taken care of, a word, etc.

Action Step

Write down your experiences, with all honesty the areas where your actions didn't align with God's will.

Closing Prayer

Close your eyes, take a deep breath, and honestly ask yourself: what wounds are you carrying that you haven't acknowledged. Let God shine a light on your hidden hurts and start the difficult, but liberating, journey of healing. Write a prayer taking ownership of your inventory.

Step Five

Admitting the truth about our struggles to God, to ourselves, and to someone we trust, allowing honesty to open the door to healing.

James 5:16a (TLB) & Romans 8:26 (TLB)

Admit your faults to one another and pray for each other so that you may be healed.

And in the same way by our faith the Holy Spirit helps us with our daily problems and in our praying. For we don't even know what we should pray for or how to pray as we should, but the Holy Spirit prays for us with such feeling that it cannot be expressed in words.

I'm Coming Clean

God, I hope you remember me, we haven't talked in so long...

I'm here to admit and confess, the exact nature of my wrongs

I'm a little numb and a little confused so I'm just gonna start...

By surrendering the scares and the failures and giving you my hardened heart

To God, myself and to another human being...

I'm admitting my wrongs..." I'm coming clean"!

Looking in the mirror it was easy to see, the raging anger in my eyes...

I had to admit to God and myself that the truth was hidden by the lies

My selfish greed was looking back at me I had to admit to myself and God...

that what I'd seen in my retched soul proved that I was a fraud

To God, myself and to another human being...

I'm admitting my wrongs..." I'm coming clean"!

So please don't judge me as I admit my wrongs, I need You to help me
through the shame...

I admit that I hate and resent the ones who caused all my pain

It's scary admitting all my wrongs and exposing my soul to another being...

But I'm letting go and I'm giving up control of my life...I'm coming clean!

To God, myself and to another human being...

I'm admitting my wrongs..."I'm coming clean"!

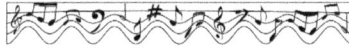

Key Themes and Song Analysis

This song highlights themes of vulnerability, self-awareness, accountability, and spiritual healing. It reflects a personal journey of honesty, confession and transformation. The key themes are:

Confession and Accountability: The song focuses on taking responsibility for one's actions and admitting past wrongs to oneself, God, and others, as emphasized in the refrain: *"I'm admitting my wrongs... I'm coming clean."*

Are you willing to admit, to yourself, that you've done wrong and that you want to make it right?

If so, make a list of some of these wrongs.

God already knows the wrongs you've done. Are you ready to confess them and ask God to forgive you? Are you willing to do that now?

How do you feel about exposing your soul by confessing your wrongs to another person?

Healing Through Honesty: There's an understanding that healing begins with confronting and expressing the truth, seen in lines like *"I had to admit to God and myself that the truth was hidden by the lies."*

Honest self-reflection and confession is essential on your journey toward healing and self-discovery. What truths have you hidden with lies?

How will honest self-reflection contribute to your journey toward healing?

Surrender and Release: The act of surrendering pain, failures, and control is a recurring theme: *"I'm letting go and I'm giving up control of my life."* This reflects trust in God for guidance and renewal. Confessing our wrongs to ourselves, God and others will bring us face to face with things we need to surrender.

Make a list of some wrongs that you need to confess, surrender and release.

How does confessing, surrendering and releasing pain, failures, and giving up control to God help in your journey towards healing and transformation?

Struggle with Shame and Vulnerability: The lyrics acknowledge the fear and shame of opening up, as in *"It's scary admitting all my wrongs and exposing my soul to another being."* This highlights the courage it takes to be vulnerable.

A person with an addiction disorder may struggle with shame, guilt and lack of self-confidence. They may also lack courage and are very vulnerable. If you struggle with any of these symptoms, it is extremely important that you choose someone that will help you overcome these struggles so that you can feel safe as you're confessing your wrongs.

Make a list of some people that you can trust with your confessions? Pick someone that you know and trust.

Seeking Forgiveness and Redemption: There is a plea for understanding and help to move through the guilt and shame, suggesting a desire for forgiveness and a fresh start: *"I need You to help me through the shame."* Forgiveness and redemption will bring healing and recovery. Guilt and shame will prevent healing and recovery.

Make a list of the things that have caused you guilt and shame and confess them. Be honest, vulnerable and repentant.

Resentment and the Path to Letting Go: The song confronts deep-seated anger and resentment toward those who caused pain, showing the internal struggle to release these feelings.

Make a list of any internal struggles (i.e., pain, rejection, hatred, abandonment etc.) that you need to surrender in your attempt to release resentment?

Pray the prayer of surrender. Father God, I give my pain, my feelings of rejection, my hatred, my abandonment to you. I take my hands off of them and give them to you. Help me not take them back but help me walk free from them. In the name of Jesus, Amen.

Spiritual Transformation: A significant spiritual theme runs through the song, with the act of confession and surrender as steps toward inner peace and transformation.

What do you need to confess and surrender on your journey towards inner peace and transformation?

How will inner peace impact your overall healing, recovery and personal growth?

Overall, the song captures a heartfelt and honest exploration of the journey toward emotional and spiritual cleansing, resonating with themes of humility, redemption, and hope.

Lectio Divina

James 5:16a (TLB) & Romans 8:26 (TLB)

Admit your faults to one another and pray for each other so that you may be healed."

And in the same way by our faith the Holy Spirit helps us with our daily problems and in our praying. For we don't even know what we should pray for or how to pray as we should, but the Holy Spirit prays for us with such feeling that it cannot be expressed in words.

Read the verse slowly and focus on each sentence. Re-read the verse a few times and try to notice different words or phrases as they jump out to you.

Reflect and meditate, take a few minutes to sit and be in that moment. Listen for that still small Voice, are there any words speaking to you?

Respond in prayer to what you heard from God and how the words spoke to you. This could be a scripture that you are praying and taking God at His word.

Rest and sit in the silence and just "be" with God for a few minutes. Write down anything that you may have heard during this time resting in His presence. It could be a promise, assurance of a matter being taken care of, a word, etc.

Action Step

In the space below start writing down your wrongs, big and small, those you've hidden from yourself and even from God. Be honest, be vulnerable, and let the peace that comes from confession wash over you.

Closing Prayer

Write a prayer admitting to God the exact nature of your wrongs, and for the Holy Spirit to help you to be completely honest with Him and yourself.

Step Six

Becoming willing for God to transform our hearts and remove attitudes, habits, and behaviors that no longer align with His will.

Romans 8:1-2 (GW)

So those who are believers in Christ Jesus can no longer be condemned. [2] *The standards of the Holy Spirit, who gives life through Christ Jesus, have set you free from the standards of sin and death.*

I'm So Ready

God I'm so ready for You to remove

My defects of character so I can improve,

I wanna stop living this lie

I've ruined and waisted so much of myself

Trying to survive without Your help,

I need You to change my life

My actions have caused so much pain

To myself, and others and I'm drowning in shame,

From living life so selfishly

I've closed the door on all of my past

I'm looking for a future that I know will last,

My soul is awake, now I believe

God I'm so ready to confess my sins...

This life I've lived has to come to an end

God I surrender so You can begin

To heal all the pain within

Oh God I'm so ready I'm so ready

For years I ran down that dead-end road...

For years I carried that heavy load

I'm giving up I'm completely spent...

I surrender, I lie down, I repent

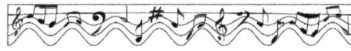

Key Themes and Song Analysis

This song centers on themes of surrender, transformation, and redemption, conveying a heartfelt plea for change and spiritual renewal. The key themes are:

Readiness for Change: The repeated declaration *"God I'm so ready"* highlights the writer's readiness to let go of their past and embrace a new way of life. A determination and commitment to let go of the past and embrace a new way of life is essential for change.

What fears have kept you from embracing change on your journey towards healing and transformation?

Are you really ready for a change? If so, what changes do you feel that you need to make?

Surrender and Repentance: The act of surrendering to God is a major theme, seen in *"I surrender, I lie down, I repent"* and the openness to God's intervention in *"I'm giving up I'm completely spent."*

Have you completely spent yourself running from God?   Are you ready to surrender and give up this madness of addiction?

If so, pray this prayer of surrender!

Father God I surrender my life to You. I give up control of my life and I'm asking you to take control of My life. In the name of Jesus, Amen.

Self-Reflection and Accountability: The writer acknowledges the pain caused by their actions, both to themselves and others, as in *"My actions have caused so much pain to myself, and others."*

How will acknowledgment of your negative actions help you heal?

How does being accountable for your negative actions, help others heal?

What is the difference between acknowledging your negative actions and being accountable for your negative actions?

Desire for Spiritual Healing: A longing for God's transformative power is evident in lines like *"I need You to change my life"* and *"To heal all the pain within."*

Do you want God's transformative power to heal your inner struggles? If so, what are some inner struggles that you need God to heal?

Letting Go of the Past: The lyrics emphasize leaving behind past mistakes and failures: *"I've closed the door on all of my past."*

What impact would closing the door on your past have on your commitment to move forward and embracing a new chapter in your life?

Make a list of things in your past that you need to close the door on.

Hope for a Better Future: There is a strong focus on hope and belief in a renewed life: *"I'm looking for a future that I know will last."* You have to see yourself in a better place before you can get to a better place.

What do you want your future to look like?

Where do you see yourself in one year?

Where do you see yourself in five years?

Acknowledgment of Personal Struggles: The song reflects on the struggles and burdens of living a self-directed life, as in *"For years I ran down that dead-end road"* and *"For years I carried that heavy load."* These lyrics illustrate the struggles and burdens of living a self-directed life.

Make a list of some of the struggles and burdens that you experienced while living a self-directed life.

What will it take to close the door on your past struggles and burdens?

Faith in Redemption: Belief in God's power to forgive and transform is central, as seen in the desire for God to *"begin to heal all the pain within."* Faith to believe in God's power to forgive and transform, is key for God to *"begin to heal all the pain within"*.

Do you have the faith to believe in God's power to heal your inner pain?

If so, make a list of the things that caused your inner pain and pray the prayer of surrender for all of them. This list may need to be updated often.

Prayer of Surrender

Father God, I surrender my inner pains to you. I take my hands off of them and I give them to You. Help me to not take them back but help me walk free from them. In the name of Jesus, Amen!

This song is a poignant and deeply spiritual narrative of moving from brokenness and despair toward surrender, faith, and hope for a new beginning.

Lectio Divina

Romans 8:1-2 (GW)

So those who are believers in Christ Jesus can no longer be condemned. [2] The standards of the Holy Spirit, who gives life through Christ Jesus, have set you free from the standards of sin and death.

Read the verse slowly and focus on each sentence. Re-read the verse a few times and try to notice different words or phrases as they jump out to you.

Reflect and meditate, take a few minutes to sit and be in that moment. Listen for that still small Voice, are there any words speaking to you?

Respond in prayer to what you heard from God and how the words spoke to you. This could be a scripture that you are praying and taking God at His word.

Rest and sit in the silence and just "be" with God for a few minutes. Write down anything that you may have heard during this time resting in His presence. It could be a promise, assurance of a matter being taken care of, a word, etc.

Action Step

Take some time to reflect on the areas of your life where you'd like to see God's transformative power at work. Be honest with yourself about the character traits you'd like to see changed and ask God to help you surrender them to Him. List those traits below and surrender them to Him.

Closing Prayer

Take time to reflect on specific character flaws you want to see God address, writing them down as a prayer list.

Step Seven

Humbly asking Jesus to heal our wounds, strengthen our character, and restore what addiction has damaged.

Romans 12:2 (NLT)

Don't copy the behavior and customs of this world, but let God transform you into a new person by changing the way you think. Then you will learn to know God's will for you, which is good and pleasing and perfect.

Humbly Asking

Now this step is a guarantee that I'm gonna lose a lot of me

By asking God to remove my shortcomings

Like resentment, self-pity, anger and fear hatred, greed, and not being
sincere

And embracing the pain that I've been numbing

Well that wasn't too bad, I thought I was done

But God said, Son you've just begun

I looked again and saw more than I wanted to like pride, denial, and
phoniness

Lying and cheating and laziness and justifying the things I over do

God I'm not good at humility but here I am down on my knees

Asking You to remove these things and help me make the change

I knew there were things still unseen I was getting weak and I was feeling
lean

And I know I have a knack for doing wrong

Like stealing, demanding, and over using being selfish, jealous, and abusing

And staying the victim for way too long

I ask God to reveal to me anything else so I could see the hidden things that
I just I couldn't find

Like guilt and shame and being crude, boastful, proud and being rude

And valuing the opinion of a sick, sick mind

God I'm not good at humility but here I am down on my knees

Asking You to remove these things and help me make the change

Key Themes and Song Analysis

This song delves into themes of self-awareness, spiritual growth, and humility. It portrays a deep commitment to confronting personal flaws and seeking divine guidance for transformation. The key themes are:

Self-Examination and Awareness: The lyrics reflect an honest and thorough inventory of personal shortcomings, as seen in the detailed listing of traits like resentment, pride, and selfishness.

How can this honest and thorough self-examination inventory of personal shortcomings contribute to your healing and transformation?

Spiritual Surrender: A key theme is the act of turning to God for help in removing these flaws, as highlighted in *"Asking You to remove these things and help me make the change."* This song highlights the act of surrendering and turning to God for help.

Make a list of the shortcomings that you need to admit you have.

Take some time and pray to surrender your shortcomings to God.

Humility: The writer acknowledges their struggle with humility and approaches God with vulnerability and sincerity: *"God I'm not good at humility, but here I am down on my knees."* Approaching God with vulnerability is the only path to healing and restoration.

Do you struggle with humility?   Write down some areas in your life that pride needs to be addressed.

Acknowledgment of Hidden Flaws: The process of uncovering deeper, less obvious shortcomings reflects a commitment to thorough self-reflection: *"The hidden things that I just couldn't find."*

Why is the process of uncovering deeper, less obvious shortcomings, so important in recovery?

We all have hidden flaws. Take a minute and ask Holy Spirit to reveal the hidden flaws in your life and write them down so you can release them to God.

Struggle and Persistence: The journey of self-improvement is portrayed as difficult and ongoing, with moments of weakness and frustration: *"I was getting weak and I was feeling lean."*

Why is the difficult and ongoing journey of self-improvement necessary for complete and lasting healing?

Make a list of some struggles that will require persistence to overcome.

Desire for Transformation: The lyrics express a longing to replace negative traits with positive change, emphasizing growth and progress.

Do you truly have the desire to replace negative traits with positive change?

If so, write down some of your negative traits that needs to be replaced with positive change.

Spiritual Guidance: A reliance on God's wisdom and power is central to the song's narrative, as the writer asks for divine revelation and support: *"I ask God to reveal to me anything else so I could see."* We all need Spiritual guidance to help us remember things that has kept us in addiction.

Take a moment and ask God for His Spiritual guidance to help you identify things that you need to overcome in your life. Write down anything that comes to mind.

Take time daily to ask God to reveal the hidden things that you need to address.

Confronting Pain and Accountability: The willingness to face and embrace pain, as well as take responsibility for past behaviors, underscores a theme of accountability. This song underscores the theme of accountability through the willingness to face and embrace pain, as well as take responsibility for past behaviors.

Make a list of the pains that you need to confront

What actions do you need to be accountable for?

This song captures the deeply personal and challenging process of spiritual and emotional growth, emphasizing humility, faith, and the transformative power of self-awareness.

Lectio Divina

Romans 12:2 (NLT)

Don't copy the behavior and customs of this world, but let God transform you into a new person by changing the way you think. Then you will learn to know God's will for you, which is good and pleasing and perfect.

Read the verse slowly and focus on each sentence. Re-read the verse a few times and try to notice different words or phrases as they jump out to you.

Reflect and meditate, take a few minutes to sit and be in that moment. Listen for that still small Voice, are there any words speaking to you?

Respond in prayer to what you heard from God and how the words spoke to you. This could be a scripture that you are praying and taking God at His word.

Rest and sit in the silence and just "be" with God for a few minutes. Write down anything that you may have heard during this time resting in His presence. It could be a promise, assurance of a matter being taken care of, a word, etc.

Action Step

Take a quiet moment to reflect on areas where you'd like to grow closer to God and ask for His help in overcoming those specific shortcomings. Write down those areas that come to mind and write a prayer asking for His help to overcome.

Closing Prayer

Take some time to reflect on the areas in your life where you feel weak or struggle. Then, pray specifically to God asking for His help in overcoming those shortcomings.

Step Eight

**Becoming willing to make things right by
making a list of those we have harmed,
as God prepares our hearts for reconciliation.**

2 Corinthians 5:18-19 (GW) & Ephesians 4:32 (TLB)

God has done all this. He has restored our relationship with Him through Christ and has given us this ministry of restoring relationships. [19] In other words, God was using Christ to restore His relationship with humanity. He didn't hold people's faults against them, and He has given us this message of restored relationships to tell others.

Instead, be kind to each other, tenderhearted, forgiving one another, just as God has forgiven you because you belong to Christ.

The List Goes On

This list will be long, it's grown over time

It tells a story of pain and heartaches

I'm making this list with one thing in mind

To make amends for the harm, caused by my mistakes

I'm going to start right here with myself

For abusing my body and destroying my mind

For riding that horse to the pits of hell

Chasing the peace that I could never find

And the list goes on!

To my children that were left behind

Forced into foster care, frightened and crying

While dad and mom were stumbling blind

Down the road of cheating and lying

And the list goes on! And the list goes on!

To my family who had to go into debt

To get me out of jail and on parole

I was so high I had no regret

I was completely out of control

And the list goes on! And the list goes on!

I've got nothing left, it's a good place to end

I know there's more, so I'll come back again

Because the list goes on! The list goes on and on, and on!

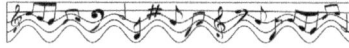

Key Themes and Song Analysis

This song revolves around themes of accountability, regret, and the on-going process of seeking forgiveness and making amends. It paints a vivid and heartfelt picture of taking responsibility for the harm caused by past actions. The key themes are:

Accountability and Acknowledgment: The writer openly admits to the mistakes and harm they have caused, demonstrating a willingness to take responsibility, as in *"To make amends for the harm, caused by my mistakes."* Acknowledging and being accountable for your actions is a choice.

Are you willing to make that choice?

In what ways does acknowledgment and accountability influence your journey toward healing, forgiveness, and personal growth?

What actions are you willing to acknowledge and be accountable for?

Regret and Remorse: There is a strong sense of regret for past actions, particularly for the pain inflicted on loved ones, such as children and family: *"To my children that were left behind... frightened and crying."*

Make a list of the people that you have hurt and the actions that you did to hurt them.

Then set a time specifically to sit down with that person, tell them what you did and make sure your regrets and remorse are sincere and ask them to forgive you.

Regret, remorse and forgiveness are sometimes not received by loved ones. What will your reaction be if your loved ones do not accept your apology and refuse to forgive you?

Self-Reflection and Growth: The song begins with the writer addressing their own self-destructive behavior: *"For abusing my body and destroying my mind."* This highlights the importance of starting the process of healing from within.

Why is it important to forgive yourself?

How does forgiving yourself influence your path towards a healthier and more fulfilling life?

Making Amends: The song's central focus is the desire to repair relationships and address past wrongs, as reflected in the recurring phrase *"And the list goes on"* This conveys both the depth of the harm and the ongoing nature of the process. Repairing relationships require you to look at and address past wrongs.

Make a list of your past wrongs and the people that they affected.

Impact on Others: The lyrics detail the ripple effects of the writer's actions on their children, family, and others, emphasizing the broader consequences of personal choices: *"To my family who had to go into debt... I was completely out of control."*

What were the impact of your actions on your family?

What were the impact of your actions on others?

Hope for Redemption: While the list is long and the process is daunting, there's an underlying hope for reconciliation and redemption through the act of making amends. The possibility of reconciliation and redemption is determined by how much damage was done to the party by your actions.

Start with those that your actions caused the least amount of damage. Make a list of these people and make amends to them first. This will give you some reconciliation to build on.

Then, work your way to those that your actions damaged the most. List those here:

Humility and Acceptance: The writer accepts that the process is not complete and will require continuous effort, as in *"I know there's more, so I'll come back again."* This demonstrates humility and a commitment to ongoing growth.

Every hurtful experience has two perspectives, the perspective of the one that was hurt and the perspective of the one who caused the hurt. And most of the time the two perspectives are very different.

Will you be willing to allow the ones you hurt to tell you what you did to hurt them without defending yourself?

Make a list of some other actions or reactions that you might need to be aware of to prepare yourself for this journey of reconciliation?

Candid Honesty: The raw, unflinching depiction of personal failures and their consequences makes the song deeply authentic and relatable.

Which lyrics retold the story of your struggles and mistakes?

How might this candid honesty influence your journey toward self-aware-ness, healing, and connection with others?

Overall, this song conveys the weight of regret but also the hope and determination to right past wrongs, embracing the long and often painful journey toward redemption and healing.

Lectio Divina

2 Corinthians 5:18-19 (GW) & Ephesians 4:32 (TLB)

God has done all this. He has restored our relationship with Him through Christ and has given us this ministry of restoring relationships. [19] In other words, God was using Christ to restore His relationship with humanity. He didn't hold people's faults against them, and He has given us this message of restored relationships to tell others.

"Instead, be kind to each other, tenderhearted, forgiving one another, just as God has forgiven you because you belong to Christ."

Read the verse slowly and focus on each sentence. Re-read the verse a few times and try to notice different words or phrases as they jump out to you.

Reflect and meditate, take a few minutes to sit and be in that moment. Listen for that still small Voice, are there any words speaking to you?

Respond in prayer to what you heard from God and how the words spoke to you. This could be a scripture that you are praying and taking God at His word.

Rest and sit in the silence and just "be" with God for a few minutes. Write down anything that you may have heard during this time resting in His presence. It could be a promise, assurance of a matter being taken care of, a word, etc.

Action Step

Write out your list to those you are reaching out to and ask the Holy Spirit to guide you in reaching out.

Closing Prayer

Reflect on your list and prayerfully consider how you can express your willingness to make amends to each person, whether through a sincere apology, a heartfelt letter, or a compassionate act of service.

Step Nine

Making amends wherever possible, guided by love, wisdom, and humility, without causing further harm.

James 5:16a (AMP) & Leviticus 6:2-4a (ERV)

*Therefore, **confess** your sins to one another [**your false steps, your offenses**], and pray for one another, that you may be healed and restored.*

*You are guilty of sin against the Lord when you do any of these things: when you lie...; when you steal something; when you cheat someone; [3] when you find something that was lost and lie about having it; when you fail to keep a promise; or when you do any other bad things like these. [4] If you do any of these things, you are guilty of doing wrong. **You must give back whatever you stole or whatever you took by cheating.***

When I Say "I'm Sorry"

I've said it so many times before,

Will anyone believe that I'm sincere

They may doubt, but the truth is

I've completed eight steps just to get here

So, I'm gonna say it again

This time it's for real

This time it's not just empty words

But it's something I really feel

Saying I'm sorry, won't get much reaction

It's not about words, it's more about action

I'm reaching out, I hope they receive it

I'm putting action to my words to help them believe it

When I say I'm sorry When I say I'm sorry

I've got to step outside of myself

Take another look, so I can see

It's not about me forgiving them

But it's about them forgiving me

I'm making amends to the ones I've hurt

I hope their wounds can heal

I know there's some that won't receive

But I know there's some that will

Key Themes and Song Analysis

This song reflects themes of sincerity, accountability, and the healing power of taking action. It focuses on the meaningful journey of seeking forgiveness and rebuilding trust. The key themes are:

Sincerity and Authenticity: The writer emphasizes that their apology is genuine and not just empty words, as highlighted in *"This time it's not just empty words, but it's something I really feel."*

How has sincerity and authenticity helped to bring meaningful change to your life?

How might this heartfelt approach to making amends help you in your journey toward healing and rebuilding trust with others?

Action Over Words: A central theme is the importance of demonstrating change through actions rather than relying solely on verbal apologies: *"It's not about words, it's more about action."* Step 8 exposed our bad actions that caused pain. Step 9 is about good actions that can bring reconciliation.

Why is action more important than words when you're trying to make amends to the people you've hurt?

What tangible steps of action are you willing to take toward rebuilding trust and restoring relationships?

Making Amends: The song portrays the process of making amends to those hurt by the writer's past actions, reflecting a commitment to reconciliation and healing: *"I'm making amends to the ones I've hurt."*

What actions are you willing to take to help restore broken relationships?

How will you make amends to those you've hurt?

Write a plan and rewrite it as you go.

Self-Awareness and Growth: The writer recognizes the need to step outside their own perspective to understand the impact of their actions: *"I've got to step outside of myself, take another look, so I can see."*

How would stepping outside of yourself, to get a different prospective, help you understand the impact your actions had on others?

How will stepping outside of yourself, to get a different prospective, help in your personal development?

Seeking Forgiveness: A strong focus is placed on the hope for forgiveness, acknowledging that it's not guaranteed but worth striving for: *"I hope their wounds can heal, I know there's some that won't receive, but I know there's some that will."*

What are your concerns about the possibility and uncertainty of not receiving forgiveness when you request forgiveness?

How will you react if someone rejects your request for forgiveness?

The Challenges of Trust and Belief: The writer confronts the doubt others may have due to their past, showing awareness of the need to rebuild trust: *"Will anyone believe that I'm sincere? They may doubt, but the truth is..."*

In what ways will this confrontation of doubt and the challenge of regaining belief from others effect your journey toward redemption?

What are you willing to do to confront doubt and rebuild trust between you and the ones that were hurt by your past actions?

People in active addiction, often do things that they don't remember. How do you feel about asking people what you did that hurt them?

Empathy and Responsibility: The lyrics highlight the importance of prioritizing the healing of those hurt over self: *"It's not about me forgiving them, but it's about them forgiving me."* In recovery you hear a lot about you forgiving others and that's important. But there comes a time when you have to start asking others to forgive you! To receive forgiveness from others you must be honest about what you did to hurt them.

Write down what you did to hurt each individual that you hurt so that you can personalize every request for forgiveness.

If you don't know what you did to hurt them don't be afraid to ask them.

Perseverance in Redemption: The repeated effort to convey sincerity and enact change shows a determination to mend relationships, even when the outcome is uncertain.

How will you react if your request for reconciliation is not accepted?

Perseverance is key to redeeming relationships. Will you be willing to try again if your first attempt for redemption is unsuccessful?

Write down what you will do if your attempt for is unsuccessful.

This song is a heartfelt exploration of taking accountability and the transformative power of genuine effort in seeking forgiveness and restoring connections. It emphasizes that true apologies are about more than words—they're about meaningful action.

Lectio Divina

James 5:16a (AMP) & Leviticus 6:2-4a (ERV)

*Therefore, **confess** your sins to one another [**your false steps, your offenses**], and pray for one another, that you may be healed and restored.*

*You are guilty of sin against the Lord when you do any of these things: when you lie...; when you steal something; when you cheat someone; ³ when you find something that was lost and lie about having it; when you fail to keep a promise; or when you do any other bad things like these. ⁴ If you do any of these things, you are guilty of doing wrong. **You must give back whatever you stole or whatever you took by cheating.***

Read the verse slowly and focus on each sentence. Re-read the verse a few times and try to notice different words or phrases as they jump out to you.

Reflect and meditate, take a few minutes to sit and be in that moment. Listen for that still small Voice, are there any words speaking to you?

Respond in prayer to what you heard from God and how the words spoke to you. This could be a scripture that you are praying and taking God at His word.

Rest and sit in the silence and just "be" with God for a few minutes. Write down anything that you may have heard during this time resting in His presence. It could be a promise, assurance of a matter being taken care of, a word, etc.

Action Step

If it's not safe or appropriate to contact those directly to make amends, consider writing a letter expressing your remorse and intention to make things right. List those individuals you are considering writing a letter to.

Closing Prayer

Lord, help me to discern the best way to make amends to those I have hurt, balancing my desire for forgiveness with protecting myself and others from further harm. Guide my words and actions so that they bring healing, not pain. And a pathway that honors both Your will and my commitment to healing.

Step Ten

Continuing daily self-reflection, promptly admitting wrongs and returning quickly to God when we fall short.

1 John 1:9 (TLB)

But if we confess our sins to Him, He can be depended on to forgive us and to cleanse us from every wrong. And it is perfectly proper for God to do this for us because Christ died to wash away our sins.

Being Sober Isn't Easy

I'm taking a personal inventory, to help me become strong

There are some things I've found, that I admit are wrong

I get so caught up in the cares of life

That I vomit anger, causing chaos and strife

My life is one big drama for all to see

When people avoid it, I think they're rejecting me

Being sober isn't easy... It's a challenge every day

Daily searching inside myself...is the only way

To peel back the layers of pain... buried in my soul

This journey is a marathon... healing is my goal

So, I continue to search, because I want to be strong!

I found some more things, that I admit are wrong!

I revisit the past where the pain began

So, I can feel like the victim again

I manipulate others to indulge myself

They don't see me again until I need something else

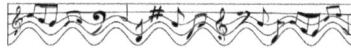

Key Themes and Song Analysis

This song explores themes of self-awareness, accountability, and the on-going journey of personal growth and healing. It provides an honest look at the struggles of maintaining sobriety and overcoming self-destructive behaviors. The key themes are:

Self-Reflection and Inventory: The writer regularly examines their thoughts and actions, acknowledging their flaws and working toward improvement: *"I'm taking another inventory, to help me stay strong."*

Are you willing to make a commitment to acknowledge your flaws and work towards self-improvement? If so, make a list of some thoughts and actions that you'll need to work on.

In what ways does this daily examination of your thoughts and actions help you stay strong'?

The Struggles of Sobriety: The song acknowledges the daily challenges of staying sober and the necessity of continuous introspection: *"Being sober isn't easy... It's a challenge every day."*

Make a list of some things that you will need to do on a regular basis to combat Triggers and Cravings?

Next, make a list of some things that you will need to stop doing on a regular basis that may be contributing to your Triggers and Cravings.

Acknowledgment of Personal Flaws: The lyrics candidly address the writer's shortcomings, such as anger, manipulation, and a tendency to revisit the past to feel victimized: *"I revisit the past where the pain began, so I can feel like the victim again."* Revisiting the past in your mind will hinder your recovery causing you to continue to feel victimized allowing pain and anger to resurface.

What can you do to stop revisiting the past? Challenge your thoughts!

Make a list of some negative thoughts that you are revisiting in your mind.

Challenge each thought with a positive thought or with a scripture from the Bible.

See Pages 123-124 about "Challenging Unhealthy Thoughts and Emotions." Pages 125-129 for a One Page exercise "Capture, Recognize, Challenge and Replace."

Impact of Emotional Pain: The layers of pain buried in the writer's soul are explored, highlighting the need for ongoing healing: *"To peel back the layers of pain... buried in my soul."*

How might the process of uncovering and addressing these deep emotional wounds influence your recovery journey towards inner healing?

Search for and make a list of the pains that may be buried deep in your soul.

Then, Surrender them to God!

Accountability and Honesty: The writer takes responsibility for their actions and behaviors, openly admitting to faults: *"And I found some more things, that I admit are wrong."*

A sincere admission of faults and taking responsibility for your actions and behaviors, are essential for a successful recovery. How might this openness and willingness to acknowledge mistakes influence your relationships with others and your path toward healing and reconciliation?

Make an honest list of things that you need to work on in your recovery.

The Desire for Growth and Healing: The ultimate goal of the writer's journey is not just sobriety but holistic healing and self-improvement: *"This journey is a marathon and healing is my goal."* It takes a long-term commitment to achieve personal growth and true inner healing.

What are some things that you feel you need to look at in your life that will help you achieve the balanced and fulfilling life of recovery?

Emotional Complexity: The song highlights the writer's struggles with feelings of rejection and the drama they perceive in their life: *"My life is one big drama for all to see, when people avoid it, I think they're rejecting me."*

Can you see yourself in this description of (drama) internal conflict within and sensitivity to perceived rejection from others? If so, make a list of some drama that was or is in your life that people may be avoiding.

Once you've delt with the drama the perceived rejection will cease.

The Cycle of Dependency: A pattern of manipulating others for self-serving purposes is acknowledged, showing a deep level of self-awareness: *"I manipulate others to indulge myself. They don't see me again until I need something else."*

Make a list of the people that you've manipulated and what you did to manipulate them.

What are some things that you can do to break the pattern of manipulating others for self-serving purposes, so you can have healthy relationships?

This song is a raw and honest exploration of the ongoing challenges and victories in the journey of sobriety, emphasizing the importance of self-awareness, accountability, and perseverance in the pursuit of personal transformation.

Lectio Divina

1 John 1:9 (TLB)

But if we confess our sins to Him, He can be depended on to forgive us and to cleanse us from every wrong. And it is perfectly proper for God to do this for us because Christ died to wash away our sins.

Read the verse slowly and focus on each sentence. Re-read the verse a few times and try to notice different words or phrases as they jump out to you.

Reflect and meditate, take a few minutes to sit and be in that moment. Listen for that still small Voice, are there any words speaking to you?

Respond in prayer to what you heard from God and how the words spoke to you. This could be a scripture that you are praying and taking God at His word.

Rest and sit in the silence and just "be" with God for a few minutes. Write down anything that you may have heard during this time resting in His presence. It could be a promise, assurance of a matter being taken care of, a word, etc.

Action Step

Take a quiet moment each day to reflect on your actions and words, seeking God's guidance to identify areas where you may have fallen short, and humbly confess your failings to Him and others.

Closing Prayer

Write a prayer for the grace to see your own shortcomings and the humility to admit fault, even in the face of judgment.

Step Eleven

Growing in our relationship with God through prayer and Scripture, seeking His guidance, peace, and power each day.

Romans 8:27 (AMP) & Colossians 1:9b (WEB)

And He who searches the hearts knows what the mind of the Spirit is, because the Spirit intercedes [before God] on behalf of God's people in accordance with God's will.

9b ...that you may be filled with the knowledge of His will in all spiritual wisdom and understanding,

Praying to Know God's Will

God I'm so scarred, from my disease

Don't know if I'm worthy of Your love for me

So, I pray and meditate, and seek to improve

My conscious contact with You...Oh God, Oh God

God help me know, Your will for me

And give me strength to pursue my destiny

So, I ask for Your power, to redeem my past

So, hope can surface at last...Oh God, Oh God

God, You know I'm selfish, God you know I've sinned

God, You know I'm weak from the demons within

But You love me anyway, so as I pray

Will You show me the way... to Your will...Oh God, Oh God

God, I won't fight, I surrender and come

Cause I know the battles already won

So, as Your love surrounds me, I come to my end

I give up, so You can begin...Oh God, Oh God, Oh God

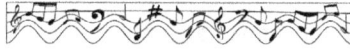

Key Themes and Song Analysis

This song is deeply spiritual, expressing themes of surrender, redemption, and the search for divine guidance and love. It captures a heartfelt journey of seeking connection with God and embracing transformation. The key themes are:

Spiritual Surrender: A central theme is the writer's act of surrendering their struggles to God, trusting in His power and plan: *"God, I won't fight, I surrender and come."*

Make a list of the battles you are fighting today?

Are you willing to surrender? If so, pray this prayer of surrender.

Father God, I surrender my battles to you. I take my hands off of them and I give them to you. Help me to not take back my battles but help me walk free from them. In the name of Jesus, Amen!

Seeking Divine Guidance: The writer desires to align with God's will, asking for clarity and strength to follow their purpose: *"God help me know, Your will for me, and give me strength to pursue my destiny."* Seeking God's guidance is one of the major themes in the 12 Steps. This spiritual longing and appeal for strength to fulfill your destiny and achieving inner peace can only be found through prayer and meditation.

What do you do on a daily basis to spend time with God?

Acknowledgment of Brokenness: The lyrics are a candid admission of the writer's struggles and imperfections, as in *"God, You know I'm selfish, God you know I've sinned."*

How might this honest admission of flaws open up a dialogue with God and help build a relationship with God?

What are some things that you need to admit to God? Be honest, He already knows!

Hope for Redemption: The writer seeks to redeem their past and find hope, believing that through God's love, healing is possible: *"So, I ask for Your power, to redeem my past, so hope can surface at last."*

Do you believe that God can heal and restore your past? If so, write down some things from your past that you want God to redeem.

Struggle with Worthiness: There's an exploration of self-doubt and feelings of unworthiness, counterbalanced by an acknowledgment of God's unconditional love: *"Don't know if I'm worthy of Your love for me... But You love me anyway."* Self-doubt and feelings of unworthiness are intertwined with addiction.

Write down scriptures that acknowledge God's unconditional love that counterbalance these feelings of unworthiness: See **Lectio Divina Scriptures on Page 118.**

Faith in God's Power: The lyrics emphasize trust in God's strength to overcome personal battles and bring renewal: *"Cause I know the battle's already won."* Trusting in God's strength is the only way to overcome personal battles and bring renewal,

Make a list of battles that you are facing or have faced.

Which battles are already won, and which ones are still being waged?

Transformation Through Divine Love: The writer expresses a desire to let go of their past and be transformed by God's presence: *"I give up, so You can begin."* Surrendering self and the desire to let go of the past to be transformed by God's presence, is the path to a new life in recovery.

What areas of your life needs to be transformed by God's love?

What do you need to give up, to be transformed through God's love?

Prayer and Meditation as Healing Practices: The importance of prayer and meditation is highlighted as a way to improve the writer's connection with God: *"So, I pray and meditate and seek to improve my conscious contact with You."*

How might the regular practice of prayer and meditation influence your path to finding inner peace and spiritual growth?

This song is a vulnerable and powerful expression of faith, acknowledging human weakness while celebrating the hope and strength found in a relationship with God. It captures the transformative journey of surrendering to divine love and guidance.

Lectio Divina

Romans 8:27 (AMP) & Colossians 1:9b (WEB)

"nd He who searches the hearts knows what the mind of the Spirit is, because the Spirit intercedes [before God] on behalf of God's people in accordance with God's will.

9b ...that you may be filled with the knowledge of His will in all spiritual wisdom and understanding,

Read the verse slowly and focus on each sentence. Re-read the verse a few times and try to notice different words or phrases as they jump out to you.

Reflect and meditate, take a few minutes to sit and be in that moment. Listen for that still small Voice, are there any words speaking to you?

Respond in prayer to what you heard from God and how the words spoke to you. This could be a scripture that you are praying and taking God at His word.

Rest and sit in the silence and just "be" with God for a few minutes. Write down anything that you may have heard during this time resting in His presence. It could be a promise, assurance of a matter being taken care of, a word, etc.

Action Step

Today set aside time for prayer and meditation focusing on connecting with God and seeking His will for your life.

Closing Prayer

Write a prayer asking for guidance in understanding His will for your life and strength to follow it.

Step Twelve

Living out this new freedom by helping others, sharing hope, and walking forward in a transformed life with Christ.

Psalm 51:12-13

Restore to me again the joy of your salvation and make me willing to obey You. [13] ***Then I will teach Your ways to others****, and they—guilty like me—will repent and return to You.*

I'll Be There for You

When your wounds just won't heal

And endless pain is all that you feel

When you're weary and desperate for rest

And you struggle for just one more breath

I've been there, made it through

And I'll be there for you!

When your nights are sleepless and long

And the urge to use is just too strong

When you need someone but no one is there

And you think that no one really cares

The road you've been on... is that road that brought me here

That road's not easy... it's hard and cold

Where happiness is just a dream and you wake up in fear

That somehow you may have already sold your soul!

I've been there, made it through

And I'll be there for you!

Key Themes and Song Analysis

This song conveys themes of empathy, shared struggle, resilience, and un-wavering support. It is a heartfelt message of solidarity and hope for those who are suffering. The key themes are:

Empathy Through Shared Experience: The writer relates deeply to the listener's pain, emphasizing that they have endured similar struggles: *"I've been there, made it through."*

On your recovery road have you experienced empathy through shared experiences? If so, write a short account of it.

How did this shared experience influence your journey towards healing, knowing that you were not alone in your challenges?

Having a sponsor and being a sponsor is critical for a healthy recovery.

Support and Encouragement: The song expresses a commitment to stand by someone in their darkest moments: *"And I'll be there for you!"*

How might our promise of being present for someone during their most challenging times bring them comfort and encouragement?

What kind of support and encouragement did you need on your recovery road?

Acknowledgment of Pain: The lyrics openly confront the raw realities of suffering, including feelings of isolation, despair, and the difficulty of recovery: *"When your wounds just won't heal, and endless pain is all that you feel."*

What were some difficult struggles with isolation and despair that you encountered in your recovery?

How does our honest portrayal of our own pain and struggles with isolation and despair help others in their recovery?

The Hardships of Addiction: Addiction is depicted as a relentless struggle, highlighting the strength needed to resist it: *"When the urge to use is just too strong."*

How did you overcome the urge to use again?

How could your experience help others overcome the urge to use?

The Challenges of Loneliness: The song acknowledges the pain of feeling abandoned and uncared for: *"When you need someone but no one is there."*

Reflect on a time when you needed someone, but no one was there. How did you make it through that experience?

Hope Amidst Adversity: Despite the hardships, the writer offers hope, showing that survival and healing are possible: *"The road you've been on... is that road that brought me here."*

In what way were you encouraged when you heard that despite the hardships, survival and healing are possible on the road to recovery?

How can your experience help others accomplish survival and healing on their road to recovery?

Reflection on the Journey of Recovery: The song emphasizes that the road to healing is not easy, but it leads to growth and resilience: *"That road's not easy... it's hard and cold."* The road of recovery brings up a lifetime of experiences in a short period of time. You relive your whole life in a few months or years, it's not easy but it leads to growth and resilience.

Take a moment to reflect on your road of recover and write down how your experiences can help others.

Reassurance of Worth: The lyrics address the fear of having lost oneself, offering reassurance that it's never too late to find hope and redemption:

"Where happiness is just a dream and you wake up in fear, that somehow you may have already sold your soul."

We end with this question. Are you willing to use your recovery experience to provide comfort and encouragement to people who believe there's no hope of reclaiming their sense of self-worth and finding redemption?

This song is a moving testament to the power of connection, hope, and mutual understanding in overcoming adversity. It offers comfort and strength to those in pain, letting them know they are not alone.

Lectio Divina

Psalm 51:12-13

*Restore to me again the joy of your salvation and make me willing to obey You. ¹³ **Then I will teach Your ways to others**, and they—guilty like me—will repent and return to You.*

Read the verse slowly and focus on each sentence. Re-read the verse a few times and try to notice different words or phrases as they jump out to you.

Reflect and meditate, take a few minutes to sit and be in that moment. Listen for that still small Voice, are there any words speaking to you?

Respond in prayer to what you heard from God and how the words spoke to you. This could be a scripture that you are praying and taking God at His word.

Rest and sit in the silence and just "be" with God for a few minutes. Write down anything that you may have heard during this time resting in His presence. It could be a promise, assurance of a matter being taken care of, a word, etc.

Action Step

Think about people in your life who might benefit from your experience with recovery and reach out to them, sharing your story and offering support.

Closing Prayer

God, I pray for the strength and courage to carry Your message of hope to others who are struggling. Help me to share my experience with them, so they to can find the freedom and peace that comes from trusting in You.

More for the Road

Lectio Divina Scriptures

Lectio Divina Worksheets

Taking Unhealthy Thoughts Captive

One-Page Exercise Worksheets

Scriptures for Lectio Divina
Prepare and Make Time
Find some alone time (mornings are good)
Find a quite place
Find some instrumental background music

Anger

Psalms 145:8	Nehemiah 9:17
Ephesians 4:26	Ecclesiastes 7:9
Psalms 37:8	Ephesians 4:31-32
Proverbs 14:17	James 1:19-20
Colossians 3:8	Romans 12:19-21

Comfort

Psalms 46:1-3	Matthew 11:28
Nahum 1:7	John 16:33
Psalms 37:24	Psalms 18:2
Psalms 55:22	Psalms 22:24

Courage

Psalms 27:14	Isaiah 43:1
Psalms 37:28	Philippians 4:12-13
Psalms 37:3	Psalms 31:24

Enemies

Psalms 37:40	Isaiah 54:17
Hebrews 13:6	2 Kings 17:39
Psalms 112:8	Psalms 27:5-6
Proverbs 16:7	Deuteronomy 20:4

Faithfulness God's

Psalms 105:8	Numbers 23:17
2 Peter 3:9	Deuteronomy 7:9
Isaiah 25:1	2 Corinthians 1:20
Psalms 89:34	Deuteronomy 4:31

Fear

Psalms 23:4-5	Isaiah 43:2
Romans 8:15	1 Peter 3:12-14
Psalms 91:4-6	John 14:27
Luke 12:32	Isaiah 41:13
Isaiah 14:3	2 Timothy 1:7

Food/Clothing Provision

Psalms 147:14	Matthew 6:24-34
Psalms 111:5	Philippians 4:19
Malachi 3:10	Psalms 81:10
Psalms 34:10	Hebrews 13:5

Forgiveness

Matthew 6:14	Matthew 5:44-45
Mark 11:25-26	Romans 12:20
Luke 6:35-38	Matthew 18:21-22

Guidance

Psalms 48:14	Isaiah 30:21
Psalms 37:23	Proverbs 16:9
Isaiah 28:26	Proverbs 3:6
Isaiah 42:16	Psalms 73:23-24

Help In Trouble

Psalms 37:39	Psalms 146:8
Psalms 22:24	Psalms 71:20
Psalms 42:11	Psalms 73:26
Psalms 28:7	Psalms 91:10-11

Hope

Psalms 42:11	Jeremiah 29:11
Romans 15:13	Romans 5:3-5
Psalms 119:114	Psalms 121:7-8
Romans 8:25	Hebrews 11:1

Humility

Psalms 10:17	Isaiah 57:15
James 4:6	1 Peter 5:6
Matthew 5:5	Matthew 18:4

Loneliness

Psalms 40:17	Numbers 23:17
Isaiah 43:4	Genesis 28:15
Isaiah 58:9	2 Corinthians 6:18

Peace

Psalms 85:8	Isaiah 57:19
John 14:27	Philippians 4:7
Isaiah 32:17	2 Thessalonians 3:16
Luke 7:50	Colossians 3:15

Self-Denial

Galatians 5:24	Matthew 16:24-36
Luke 18:29-30	Romans 8:12-13

Sin, Freedom From

Romans 6:11	Romans 6:1-2
Romans 6:14	Romans 6:6-7
Acts 10:43	2 Corinthians 5:1

Trust

Psalms 37:3-5	Psalms 84:11-12
John 6:35,47	Proverbs 3:5-6
Isaiah 32:17	2 Timothy 3:14-15
John 3:18,36	Galatians 3:26

Lectio Divina

Prayer is Talking with God   Meditation is Listening to God

Scripture to Meditate On:

Read the verse slowly and focus on each sentence. Re-read the verse a few times and try to notice different words or phrases as they jump out to you.

Reflect and meditate, take a few minutes to sit and be in that moment. Listen for that still small Voice, are there any words speaking to you?

Respond in prayer to what you heard from God and how the words spoke to you. This could be a scripture that you are praying and taking God at His word.

Rest and sit in the silence and just "be" with God for a few minutes. Write down anything that you may have heard during this time resting in His presence. It could be a promise, assurance of a matter being taken care of, a word, etc.

Lectio Divina

Prayer is Talking with God   Meditation is Listening to God

Scripture to Meditate On:

Read the verse slowly and focus on each sentence. Re-read the verse a few times and try to notice different words or phrases as they jump out to you.

Reflect and meditate, take a few minutes to sit and be in that moment. Listen for that still small Voice, are there any words speaking to you?

Respond in prayer to what you heard from God and how the words spoke to you. This could be a scripture that you are praying and taking God at His word.

Rest and sit in the silence and just "be" with God for a few minutes. Write down anything that you may have heard during this time resting in His presence. It could be a promise, assurance of a matter being taken care of, a word, etc.

Lectio Divina

Prayer is Talking with God   Meditation is Listening to God

Scripture to Meditate On:

Read the verse slowly and focus on each sentence. Re-read the verse a few times and try to notice different words or phrases as they jump out to you.

Reflect and meditate, take a few minutes to sit and be in that moment. Listen for that still small Voice, are there any words speaking to you?

Respond in prayer to what you heard from God and how the words spoke to you. This could be a scripture that you are praying and taking God at His word.

Rest and sit in the silence and just "be" with God for a few minutes. Write down anything that you may have heard during this time resting in His presence. It could be a promise, assurance of a matter being taken care of, a word, etc.

Lectio Divina

Prayer is Talking with God   Meditation is Listening to God

Scripture to Meditate On:

Read the verse slowly and focus on each sentence. Re-read the verse a few times and try to notice different words or phrases as they jump out to you.

Reflect and meditate, take a few minutes to sit and be in that moment. Listen for that still small Voice, are there any words speaking to you?

Respond in prayer to what you heard from God and how the words spoke to you. This could be a scripture that you are praying and taking God at His word.

Rest and sit in the silence and just "be" with God for a few minutes. Write down anything that you may have heard during this time resting in His presence. It could be a promise, assurance of a matter being taken care of, a word, etc.

Challenge Unhealthy Thoughts and Emotions

1 Corinthians 13:11 (NLT)

When I was a child, I spoke and thought and reasoned as a child. But when I grew up, I put away childish things.

Many addiction experts agree that if a person doesn't deal with immature emotional behaviors and thoughts, they are setting themselves up for physical relapse.

A life in active addiction is lived with unhealthy emotions, thoughts (unhealthy self-talk) and behaviors learned as a child. Unhealthy thoughts and emotions can be but not limited to: anger, rage, stress, fear, anxiety, shame, hate, regret, and anything that makes you "lose it", reacting to an event or situation instead of responding.

Healthy emotions are responding to situations in your life with thought and taking time to look at the situation from all perspectives. God has provided a way to overcome unhealthy thoughts, emotions, and behaviors. It's believing what the Bible says about what He thinks about you and the hope for your future He has for you.

So how do you deal with these immature and unhealthy thoughts, emotions, and behaviors? By challenging your unhealthy thoughts and emotions. By challenging your unhealthy thoughts and emotions you are taking back control!

Challenge Unhealthy Thoughts and Emotions

Romans 12:2 (EASY)

Do not become like the people who belong to this world. But let God completely change the way that you think, so that you live differently. Then you will understand what God wants you to do. You will know what is good. You will know what pleases God. You will know what is completely right.

Let's look at a list of Emotions:

Common Emotions

Anger	Grief	Resentful
Anxiety	Guilt	Self-conscious
Bored	Insecure	Shame
Confused	Irritated	Suspicious
Depression	Jealous	Tense
Discontent	Lonely	Terrified
Embarrassed	Loss	Trapped
Envious	Miserable	Uncomfortable
Fear	Overwhelmed	Worry
Frustration	Rage	Worthless

Before you **react to a situation** try this one page exercise:

Taking Unhealthy Thoughts Captive

Write down the Event/Situation - The Facts!

Write down the event in facts not your feelings about the event. Think and write it down before you act, respond don't react.

Capture - Hearing Yourself Talk (Self-Talk)

Capture - write down what you are hearing in your head. (Unhealthy Self-Talk)

Recognize - My Unhealthy Thoughts

Recognize – the Unhealthy Thought and Emotion (Is it Anger, Rage, Fear, Panic, etc. Are you acting out? What is your behavior?)

Challenge - Unhealthy Thoughts with Facts

Challenge - the Unhealthy Thought and Emotion with the Truth/Fact.

Replace - Unhealthy Thoughts with Healthy Thoughts

Unhealthy Thoughts	Healthy Thoughts

Replace – with Healthy Thoughts and Emotions.

Hope, Gratitude, Thankfulness, Acceptance, Peace, Joy, Gladness, and Caring.

Prayer and Meditation can help with this list.

Taking Your Unhealthy Thoughts Captive

Write down the Event/Situation - The Facts!

Capture: Hearing Yourself Talk (Self-Talk)

Recognize: My Unhealthy Thoughts

Challenge: Unhealthy Thoughts with Facts

Replace: Unhealthy Thoughts with Healthy Thoughts

Taking Your Unhealthy Thoughts Captive

Write down the Event/Situation - The Facts!

> [empty box]

Capture: Hearing Yourself Talk (Self-Talk)

> [thought cloud]

Recognize: My Unhealthy Thoughts

> [bracketed area]

Challenge: Unhealthy Thoughts with Facts

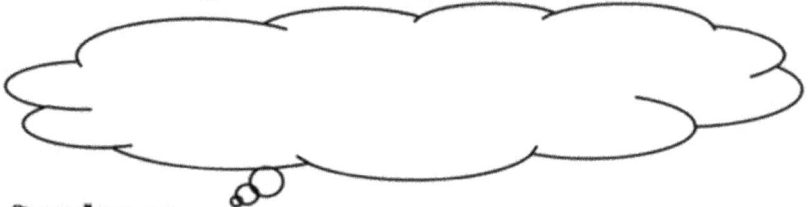

> [thought cloud]

Replace: Unhealthy Thoughts with Healthy Thoughts

> [empty rounded box]

Taking Your Unhealthy Thoughts Captive

Write down the Event/Situation - The Facts!

Capture: Hearing Yourself Talk (Self-Talk)

Recognize: My Unhealthy Thoughts

Challenge: Unhealthy Thoughts with Facts

Replace: Unhealthy Thoughts with Healthy Thoughts

Taking Your Unhealthy Thoughts Captive
Write down the Event/Situation - The Facts!

Capture: Hearing Yourself Talk (Self-Talk)

Recognize: My Unhealthy Thoughts

Challenge: Unhealthy Thoughts with Facts

Replace: Unhealthy Thoughts with Healthy Thoughts

Acknowledgements

To those who helped bring the 12 Steps to life, a heartfelt thank you.

To Steve Dady, your vision and ear for detail are the reason these songs sound the way they do. You pushed me, challenged me, and made sure I never settled for anything less than my best. Thank you!

To Nashville's dream team Dave Cleveland, Jason Webb, Blair Masters, Dan Needham, Garth Justice, Gary Lunn, Chris Donohue, background vocalist Melodie Kirkpatrick and Terry White all of you brought your God given talent and energy on every track, thank you. It was a joy to collaborate with you.

To John Heindrich, a huge thank you to for believing in this project giving your time and talent to bring the demo to life.

To Pastor Mat Varni and Potter's House Church Family the seed that was planted for our ministry was water and cultivated there, thank you for allowing it to flourish. We are deeply grateful for your support.

At last but not least to Cindy and Doug McMordie our dear friends who were there in the very beginning of our ministry thank you for not just believing in us, but for believing in My Recovery Road with your financial support. Your friendship and prayers means more than words can express.

About the Authors

John and Bridget, have walked a road paved with both faith and experience. This duo fueled by faith and a passion for helping others, embarked on their ministry journey in 2003 as Licensed Ordained Ministers with the International Church of the Foursquare Gospel. From the Texas plains to the Tennessee hills, they served as pastors, guiding and supporting their congregations. But their hearts yearned to reach beyond the church walls, to touch lives that were hurting and broken. They took a powerful step forward, educating and equipping themselves as Peer Recovery Specialists in Tennessee, enabling them to offer direct, empathetic support to individuals struggling with mental illness, substance use disorder, or co-occurring conditions.

In 2019, they birthed My Recovery Road Media Group, a beacon of hope for those seeking a life beyond addiction. Through their eMagazine publications, books, music, and ministry events, they offer a lifeline of encouragement, practical tools, and unwavering support. My Recovery Road empowers individuals with faith-based resources to navigate their recovery journeys, building confidence and strength every step of the way. John and Bridget are living proof that compassion, faith, and a shared human experience can create a pathway to healing and hope.

THANK YOU FOR YOUR PURCHASE!

BOOK STORE

For faith-based recovery
books, planners, devotional
and music check out
My Recovery Road's Bookstore

myrecoveryroad.com/shop
johnlippard.com
or Amazon

www.ingramcontent.com/pod-product-compliance
Lightning Source LLC
Chambersburg PA
CBHW060804050426
42449CB00008B/1532